Dream Sender

Southern Messenger Poets
DAVE SMITH, SERIES EDITOR

Other Books by David Huddle

POETRY

Glory River
Grayscale
Summer Lake: New and Selected Poems
The Nature of Yearning
Stopping by Home
Paper Boy
Blacksnake at the Family Reunion

FICTION

Nothing Can Make Me Do This
La Tour Dreams of the Wolf Girl
Not: A Trio—A Novella and Two Stories
The Story of a Million Years
Tenorman
Intimates
The High Spirits: Stories of Men and Women
Only the Little Bone
A Dream with No Stump Roots in It
A David Huddle Reader
The Faulkes Chronicle

ESSAYS

The Writing Habit

Dream Sender

POEMS

DAVID HUDDLE

Louisiana State University Press   *Baton Rouge*

Published by Louisiana State University Press
Copyright © 2015 by David Huddle
All rights reserved
Manufactured in the United States of America
LSU Press Paperback Original
First printing

DESIGNER: Michelle A. Neustrom
TYPEFACE: Arno Pro

The author thanks the journals in which some of these poems appeared: *Appalachian Heritage:* "Even Then I Knew" and "Evidence Contributing to a Illumination"; *Birchsong: Poetry Centered in Vermont:* "The Call"; *Connotation Press: An Online Artifact:* "Even Then I Knew," "Homothology," and "Sex Sentence"; *The Nervous Breakdown:* "Epiphany in the Parking Lot"; *Plume:* "Bear and the Crows," "The Dancers Speak of God," "God Speaks of Dancers," "Gun Notes," and "What is Unknown"; *Shenandoah:* "Bear Goes Metaphysical" and "Strangers at Twilight"; *Subtropics:* "Wren and Bear."

The author is especially grateful to James Diehr for the use of a detail from his sculpture *Dream Sender,* which served as the inspiration for the title poem of this book.

LIBRARY OF CONGRESS CATALOGING-IN-PUBLICATION DATA

Huddle, David, 1942–
  [Poems. Selections]
  Dream sender : poems / David Huddle.
    pages ; cm. — (Southern Messenger Poets)
  ISBN 978-0-8071-6013-8 (pbk. : alk. paper) — ISBN 978-0-8071-6014-5 (pdf) — ISBN 978-0-8071-6015-2 (epub) — ISBN 978-0-8071-6016-9 (mobi)
  I. Title.
  PS3558.U287A6 2016
  811'.54—dc23

                                                      2015000306

The paper in this book meets the guidelines for permanence and durability of the Committee on Production Guidelines for Book Longevity of the Council on Library Resources. ∞

For Meighan Sharp and Amy Wright

Contents

1. DOMESTIC STRANGE

Concert 3
Service 4
Cardinal Rules 5
Shot at Costco 6
The Ten Thousand Errors 7
Blinds 8
Embrace 9
I Reckon 10
I Reckon Again 11
Stores 12
Okay 13
Bon Voyage 14
Self Therapy 15
Solidarity 16
Dead Friends 17
Fountain of Old Age 18
Gun Notes 19

2. DREAM SENDER

What Is Unknown 25
Scrap Wood 31
Dream Sender 32
No Where 33
Genital Epistemology 34
Sex Sentence 35
Wren & Bear 37
Bear Goes Metaphysical 39
Bear and the Crows 41
God Speaks of Dancers 42
The Dancers Speak of God 42

How It Works 44
Sit With It 45
The Greatness of Teddy Wilson 46
Practice 47

3. THE BAT

The Call 51
Evidence Contributing to a Late
    Illumination 53
Even Then I Knew 55
Meditation 57
Epiphany in the Parking Lot 59
Dog Sutra 60
Okay #2 61
Against Auld Lang Syne 62
My Father Breathing 63
Witness 64
A Little Drunk 65
Then 70
Real Lady 71
The Uplift Obligation 72
Comes a Moment 73
Homothology 74
When the Bat Goes to Live with Jesus 75

1

Domestic Strange

do-mes-tic

1. of or pertaining to the home, the household, household affairs, or the family: domestic pleasures.
2. devoted to home life or household affairs.
3. tame; domesticated.
4. of or pertaining to one's own or a particular country as apart from other countries: domestic trade.
5. indigenous to or produced or made within one's own country; not foreign; not foreign: domestic goods.

strange

1. unusual, extraordinary, or curious; odd; queer: a strange remark to make.
2. estranged, alienated, etc., as a result of being out of one's natural environment: In Bombay I felt strange.
3. situated, belonging, or coming from outside of one's own locality; foreign: to move to a strange place; strange religions.
4. outside of one's previous experience; hitherto unknown; unfamiliar: strange faces; strange customs.
5. unaccustomed to or inexperienced in; unacquainted (usually followed by to): I'm strange to this part of the job.

—Dictionary.com

Concert

Drumming rocks our neighborhood most afternoons:
A college kid in a basement apartment,
tactful as drummers go, generates a not
unpleasant rhythmic undercurrent
for yard work, wandering the house, reading,
typing, having a snack. It's a sound track

that transports our hero to his school band
practicing Sousa marches, then makes him dance
around the dining room in remembrance
of Charlottesville frat parties. Now he's in
the kitchen, playing the counter like Ray Charles,
and look, the camera's zooming in—he's

staring out the window, seeing how his life
sweeps him there to here and won't turn him loose.

Service

An old man who buys flowers for the house,
I find the right vase, cut their stems, fix them
to generate happiness in the heart
of anyone glancing their way. Sweetheart
roses this morning in the dining room

revise my problematic history.
No prize as a young husband, I'll be buying
bouquets on into my nineties. A trick
I've learned is to water these posies daily,
fluff and spritz them, cheer them up on their way

to dropping their petals. Did I say I'm retired,
seventy-one, a grandpa, and don't want
a long life? See how nimbly my fingers
spruce these babies up? I want my flowers now.

Cardinal Rules

Half light's what cardinal and his wife like
best, so dawn and twilight those two are first
and last birds of the day,
                              Mr. Brazen
and Ms. Subtle, where there's one the other's
likely to be nearby, monogamous

I guess, and sometimes he'll pick up a seed
and place it in her beak, damned saccharine
if you ask me.
                   Cardinals don't fly
in flocks like crows and sparrows. They do sing
though it's far from melodious.
                                Not dear
like a wren, not a bully like a nuthatch,
not elusive like a warbler, not sociable
like a chickadee.
                   A girl once told me
she was pretty sure cardinals are Catholic.

Shot at Costco

Small room, bright lights, a desk, two chairs—I take it
upon myself to close the door, strip off
my green shirt and my purple shirt, then sit
in the corner chair. So quiet in here.
Alone in my undershirt, I've committed no
crime, I'm just waiting.
                            A tall young woman
in a white coat enters with a small tray
and a red plastic half-gallon jug. She kneels
beside me. We make a burst of small talk
while she swabs the fat of my upper arm,
pierces the skin, plunges in the juice, pulls

out and tosses the syringe into the jug.
You're fast, I say. She's out the door hummingbird
quick. I dress, leave, go about my business.

The Ten Thousand Errors

On any given day the average adult
commits from fifty to several hundred
unnoted mistakes, little drops, burns,
paper cuts, losses, stumbles, bumps,
misplacements, typos, trips, overturns,
forgets, swerves, skids, misremembers,
toe-stubs, misinterpretations, wrongful
statements, confusions, slips, wardrobe mix-ups,
errors of judgment, zigs instead of
zags, math mistakes, insensitive remarks,
unbuttoned buttons, open flies, and inadvertent
revelations of basic idiocy. Hey, you
klutz, train wreck, complete mess!
How about lunch later today?

Blinds

Up for me, down for Lindsey, so this one
                        particular evening I don't like how
vigorously she pulls them all the way down
              to the floor, but over the years I've trained
myself to stifle such thoughts, or maybe
                  I should say she and I have enlightened
my inner dictator as to the patriarchy,
      marital politics, and how one person's wrong
can be another's right, so I say nothing,
       and mostly forget the blinds until next morning
when I try to raise them and they're stuck
            in the down position and it's Lindsey's fault,
which makes me despicably happy
                  until hours later when I try pulling
the cord in the other direction,
              and they go up just fine, which is
exactly when I know I'll be keeping
                this little drama all to myself.

Embrace

    for Lindsey

When we put our heads together like this
I give you the sight of my face as others
rarely see it. Well, my dermatologist

uses bright lights and a magnifying glass
as she and I chat. My insurance reimburses
her for getting together with me like this.

I don't think of her when you and I kiss,
and I don't think of you when I'm with her,
I'm just glad you're not my dermatologist.

With you it's a whole lifetime experience.
We've been doing this for what, forty years?
We completely know each other's faces.

Liquid nitrogen, electric needles,
scalpels—she's not without her resources—
it can be intense at my dermatologist's.

Is there anybody alive now who remembers
how pretty our young faces were, my dear?
Yes, we put our heads together like this—

I Reckon

I who like to think money's no big deal
have never been without food or a bed.
Once on a dare I shoplifted a candy bar,
I picked up money someone dropped beside a car
and furtively stuffed the cash in my pocket
while checking to see if I'd been observed.

Once reported by a custodian for kicking
a soda machine until it barfed out
three or four dollars in change, I was called
in by my boss to explain myself. Trembling
with indignation, my voice told him
that numerous times that same machine

had kept my money and given me nothing.
I wanted him to tell me I was right
or I was wrong, but he just sighed and flapped
his hand toward the door to get rid of me.

I Reckon Again

I come from a long line of good citizens—
one crazy aunt, one dope-addict brother
but nobody who ever went to jail.
My father, my grandfather, and I followed
our moderately successful Dutch
and Scotch ancestors.
                              But who I admired
in high school was John Sharp, leather collar
turned up in a cold wind, pegged jeans, black hair
slicked back, cigarette cupped so Coach couldn't
see it if he drove by, Johnny leaning
on a parking meter, knowing they wouldn't
take him to court or kick him out of school
until after football season was over
after which he could give a shit less.

Stores

Fifteen I got a job at Leggett's, stock
boy, fifty cents an hour. Moved up—I come
from that kind of people—to Toys at Christmas,
then Menswear and finally Shoes.
                                              Quit to go
to college, never worked retail again, but
I still really like stores, savor merchandise
neatly stacked on tables, sweaters wanting
my gliding palm as I walk by, mannequins
weirdly sexy behind big glass windows,
shoes shiny and just waiting for the right feet.

So why in my seventies do Target, Lowes,
and Home Depot spin me dizzy and lost,
wanting my mother to find me, wipe my eyes,
hold my hand all the way out to the car?

Okay

I'm a little depressed, but please don't call
a shrink, I just need to snoop around in these
shadows a while, a necessary perspective
I want to take advantage of now that
it's here, an old motel where everything's
slightly strange, no TV, and all the light bulbs
are twenty-five watts or less.
                                        Call-the-shrink-
depressed is loading the shotgun in the car
to head for the woods when you're not a hunter
or sitting with your back to the window
all day, and not even noticing you've
peed your pants.
                      Soon enough I'll be Mister
Cheerful. Meanwhile I'm taking this class
for credit at the University of Twilight.

Bon Voyage

Entering that familiar capsule
we're inoculated by something so
potent we'd scream like an infant getting
a shot if the thought didn't pierce our minds
so quickly we hardly notice:
                                  Brother
and sister travelers, maybe we will be
final companions today, spending our last
seconds plummeting together. I suspect
we won't pray or sing, but some few of us
will hold hands, others may meet the eyes
of a seatmate.
                    Our lives have been mostly good,
don't you think? I don't know you, dear stranger,
but I'd rather have you with me than go
down alone. As deaths go, this one won't be so bad.

Self Therapy

How it is now is how I think it's going
to be forever. Gloomy rain now same
thing tomorrow the day after and on
and on. Stupid I know but it's just how
I came into this soggy old world. Can't
see beyond my moods either—full of beans
now, well then probably on my deathbed
I'll act the fool and tell ridiculous
lies about the grave digger. Limited
in vision, unreliable in thought,
I counsel myself as best I can. *This
won't last*, says my interior shrink. *New
day's on the way. Shut up*, I say. *I've lived
well and been wrong about nearly everything.*

Solidarity

    for K. A.

When I think of you I'm stopped in my thoughts,
a sudden sight of your shy, rueful smile
that tells how you stood up from bed this morning
and pushed through the heavy sadness that weighed
you down, that tried to hold you still, stop the breath
in your chest. So very hard to bathe and dress,
to make tea, put jam on toast, step outside
and accept sunlight, cool air, even lilacs.
Another ordinary day treating us
like guests! That breeze's pleasuring our skin
can be almost unbearable, friends so dear
we could weep for how much we care for them.
Yes, it fills us with joy. But it hurts, too.
Makes us want to curl into sleep and stay there.

Dead Friends

    for T. A. B. and J. D. E.

Don't get too close to me, the Reaper's
keeping track of who I can't do without
and scything them down. In Respite House
I sat with Alan on his next-to-last day.
Never opened his eyes or stirred, just breathed

very slowly while I gazed out his window
at trees, clouds, sunlight, and goldfinches,
sifting through forty years of friendship.

I took my new camera to John's house
a week before his surgery. In pain
and scared he was himself enough to show
bemused contempt for my new toy.
                                        I got just
one of him grinning in his Green Bay cap,
my old pal, trying his best to look jaunty.

Fountain of Old Age

Who can afford a couple thousand bucks
for a nonessential item orders
a four-hundred pound polished black granite
fountain to be shipped from New Mexico
to his backyard in Vermont. This money

could have been weeks of a grandchild's college
education. This fountain pumps water up
from a basin beneath it into a plume
of silver that trickles back down to be
pumped up again. The old buyer loves

how the water slips down the boulder's smooth
round sides. Some nights he goes out for a visit
under the stars. Eyes and ears not so good,
he stands close. He'd trade places with that stone.

Gun Notes

    1.

This man and I softly discussed hunting
at a dinner party. I'd just met him,
we'd liked each other immediately,
but we spoke carefully, as nowadays
men must do who aren't looking to argue.

I asked if he'd advise me on a matter
that'd been nagging me: I owned a shotgun
but had lost track of where the ammunition
was in the house, and I'd become concerned
about defending myself and my wife

in case of a break-in. Should I buy shells
for the gun was my question. My new friend
had tales to tell of tragic accidental
shootings and near shootings. Finally, though,

    2.

he said yes, buy the shells. Then I asked if
I should load the shotgun—it's a ladies'
.410 gauge side-by-side my grandfather bought
for my grandmother that she had never fired.
Clayton—that's his name—said, *Definitely not,*

put the box of shells high up in the closet
where you keep the gun. This was wise advice.
Clayton and I both knew if intruders
broke in, it'd be unlikely I could fetch
the box down, pluck out the shells, and load them

in time to confront the perps with my antique
shotgun, and even if I could have, would that
have been what I wanted? We both knew
I just needed a way to pretend I was safe.

   3.
Datillio's Gun Shop & Gas Station
holds three young men, a leathery old codger,
and a boy about twelve, surrounded
by displays of archery equipment,
towering shelves of ammunition, pistols
beneath glass cases, rifles and shotguns
on racks above and behind the counter
—and it's still a working filling station!

All five males scrutinize me steadily
when I say what I want. They listen to me
describing the shotgun to the one
wearing camouflage, who asks me what size
shells I have in mind. The six of us determine
two-inch shells are what I should buy. Small, heavy
box in my hand, weirdly validated,
I walk out into November's fading light.

   4.
Twilight when I get home, house to myself,
I unsheathe Grandmama Huddle's shotgun
from its canvas case to carry it downstairs,
to reckon with it in the family room.

I'd forgotten how a gun in my hand
unmoors me, turns me into somebody
capable of I don't know what. Here
with a TV, a rocking chair, toys, books

a poinsettia, I fool with my weapon.
I open it, squint down the empty barrels,
load and unload the shells, switch the safety
on and off. In this room I don't raise the gun

to my shoulder, nestle it against my cheek,
place my finger on the trigger. Wrong to do that.

   5.

My childhood home had rifles from three wars
mounted on its walls; a snub-nose .38
stashed in a bureau drawer underneath
my father's socks; air rifles and pellet guns
in closets and back rooms. I adored the cap guns
and holsters Santa Claus brought me for Christmas.
I once pointed an empty BB gun
at my brother's ear and pulled the trigger.
I've hunted deer, shot birds and rabbits.
Most days in the army I carried a rifle
or a pistol.
          The twenty first graders shot
in Newtown made me want never to see
another gun. Those dead kids, shot again
and again, made me want to kill somebody.

   6.

Violence-addicted gun-idiot
America, I'd shed you like a rattlesnake
scraping off its old skin except I'd still
be a rattlesnake.
          My wife and I said
we'd move to Canada if George Bush was
elected a second time, and he was,
and we didn't.

     We had our excuses,
still have them, but we could leave today if
we really wanted to, if we weren't
who we are,
      believers like our parents
and theirs,
      citizens blind to what we do—
kill our children, shame and imprison our poor,
dishonor our old folks, and make our crooks rich.

I have a gun in my house. Don't fuck with me.

2
Dream Sender

What Is Unknown

1.

When I tell her I've fallen for What Is Unknown, my mother's face brightens. "She'll be a good girlfriend for you," my mother says. "Not stuck up like that trashy Well Known. Not boring like that awful Perfectly Well Known. Bring her here for spaghetti on Wednesday night. We'll see what your father thinks about her." Then she turns to me with a shy smile. "I wonder what your children will look like," she says.

2.

On our first date What Is Unknown and I drive up to Lexington to see the Civil War graveyard. Later we'll go to the Southern Restaurant for dinner. In the car she doesn't have much to say, but she smiles at me every time I glance over at her. I get a notion to reach over and take her hand. My thought makes me start imagining that's exactly what she'd like—me to reach over there. I want to. I can almost feel her wanting me to. I raise my hand and will it over toward What Is Unknown. It doesn't make it that far. It settles on the console between us. It taps its fingers.

3.

In the library, What Is Unknown likes to stroll along the aisles between the shelves, sliding her fingers along the spines of the books as she walks. She hums while she sashays down the aisle, and it seems fine with her that I follow along behind. "Stop looking at my butt," she instructs me one afternoon. Her voice is mildly hostile. "Actually, I'm savoring the elegant way your neck curves down to become your shoulders," I say. "You're lying," she says. But now her tone is sociable. "Well, yes," I say.

4.

I really like reading aloud to What Is Unknown. She plops herself down on the sofa, then I stretch out with my head in her lap. I put a book on a pillow on my stomach—she lets me read any one I want. She sits so still and quiet that I might suspect her of napping except that now and then she strokes my forehead while I read. She knows I like the touch of her fingers even though

I don't stop reading. The back of my head has grown extremely fond of her upper thigh—the right one. I don't think we've ever switched sides of the sofa. Over time the back of my head and What Is Unknown's upper right thigh have become cozier than has been possible for other parts of our bodies. I'm okay with this. I don't know what What Is Unknown thinks about it.

5.

"You blather," What Is Unknown announces to me one morning at breakfast. This is soon after we start living together. "I know," I murmur. "I can't help it when I'm around you. I feel like I have to keep talking, even though I don't really have anything to say." What Is Unknown has been girding herself for an argument, but now I've made her point for her. She smiles enigmatically just before she slurps the last of the milk straight from her cereal bowl. "I'll probably get used to it," she murmurs as she carries her bowl and spoon to the sink. Leaving the kitchen, she lightly fist-bumps me on the shoulder. Like I'm her little brother.

6.

"Please talk with me about death," I ask her. It's late afternoon. We're in the graveyard. The stones make long shadows. This is where I always prefer to go with What Is Unknown when we take our walks. She seems to like it up here, too, except that she becomes just so darn reticent. "I really need some discussion of this topic," I tell her. She steps close, places her hands on my shoulders and gives me one of her up-on-tiptoes lightest-of-kisses that gets me so worked up my face feels like it's going to start sprouting zits any second. Then she pushes away and beams her smile into my face. "Let's read some of these gravestones, okay?" she says. "I love these goofy old things," she says.

7.

What Is Unknown has become quite excited about the new fuck-me fashions. She has a way of strutting along the sidewalk in her tiny skirts and heels that makes me very proud to be walking beside her. Both men and women look at her with obvious desire, but I'm the one whose arm she's holding. Truth is, if she weren't using me to help keep her balance she'd fall on her face. But then the secret truth is that I might as well be cohabiting with a Mother Superior.

"Please," she tells me after we've gone to bed and I'm creeping my fingers along the hem of her nightgown. "I can't do that," she says. "Don't be a dick," she says.

8.

What Is Unknown is nuts about the bunnies that appear at the edge of the meadow just at dusk. She paces very slowly toward them, singing softly as she takes her steps, *Oh, little bunny, I can't see you, yes, you're invisible, just keep sitting still.* But when the bunny breaks for cover she gives chase for a couple of strides, laughing raucously. "It's their little cotton tails that I want," she says. "Gonna catch one of them by its tail one of these evenings." I indulge her in her antics because whenever she sees one or more of those bunnies it puts her in a grand mood. But I also wonder if What Is Unknown really is as simpleminded as she appears to be on these bunny occasions. I always check out the surrounding area to see who might be watching us.

9.

Sometimes What Is Unknown recites to me stories and poems that have not yet been written. Sometimes songs, though she's reluctant to sing them because she knows I consider the new music inferior to the old. "You're the proverbial mud with a stick in it," she tells me. I know she's just teasing. "How about a whole novel?" I ask. "I could listen to you for days on end." She gives me a funny look and starts to say something but changes her mind. "Okay," she says. She stares up at the ceiling a moment, then clears her throat. "An awful man came to town and started burning down the churches," she begins. "His dutiful wife assisted him." She recites this novel for nineteen hours straight, and because of her lilting contralto voice I take in every word. Later, however, after I've finally gotten some sleep, I can't remember anything about the novel. I only know what What Is Unknown's voice sounded like while she was reciting. First taste of birthday cake. Cold water when you're thirsty.

10.

When I discover that What Is Unknown likes walking out into the field on slightly chilly and very clear nights, we suddenly have a sex life. Albeit one with a certain amount of discomfort. "I just like the stars," she says, "and the moon does something to me." We're halfway through October, and she's shivering. "I shouldn't let you take advantage of me the way you do." But her voice is low and sweet when she says it. Her smile makes it clear she's very pleased that I've finally gotten past first base. I give her a look of my own. "A heh heh heh," I say. "Oh, you!" she says, gives me a soft cheek-smack that turns into a caress. I know better than to suggest that we go indoors. When we're in the house she's somebody else.

11.

"Do you mind if I call you What?" I ask. What Is Unknown's eyes flash at me before she turns away. She presses her lips together. Who'd have thought such a plain question would hurt her feelings? "Okay, okay," I say, "I was just wondering. I really actually like your whole name. All four syllables." I tap her wrist, but she flings my hand away. "What you don't understand," she tells me in this raspy voice that is strange to my ears, "is that I was here before time or darkness or light. I was here before trees and clouds and birds. I come from a place that is beyond your capacity even to imagine. Watch this!" She snaps her fingers and a bolt of lightning blasts out a pit from the sidewalk directly beside me. When I jump, it feels like I'm going to be swallowed up by the great clap of thunder that billows out above us. "Okay, okay," I say. "I'm sorry," I say. She folds her arms. "What's my name?" she asks.

12.

"Why do you hang out with me?" I whisper across the table. We're having dinner at the Trattoria, her favorite place. She's all gussied up and looks killer-beautiful. Her eyes are especially luminous this evening. People all over the restaurant keep glancing over at us. Well, of course it's What Is Unknown they're eyeballing, but I know what they're thinking—which is why I ask her the question. I smile at her to suggest that I'm just being sociable. She cocks her head and grins. "Good question," she says and forks another bite of her saltimbocca. Maybe she's really into her food or maybe she's just not going to even try to give me an answer. "There are lots of men more interesting than I am," I say. I really want to hear what she has to say on this point. "That's true," she says. She's chewing when she says it. She looks at me with bemusement and affection. Maybe she's so into me that the question seems silly to her. Or maybe she's on the verge of informing me that she's cutting me loose. "That's very true," she says.

13.

When What Is Unknown and I have sex we try to describe for each other what it feels like. We like to have these conversations during the act itself. Sometimes I suspect us of having the sex just so we can have the conversation. *I'm lava that's been heating up and holding still for a thousand years. Now all of a sudden there's movement, there's a way out, we're on our way! No hurry, mind you, but we're going to get there. I'm an old turkey buzzard just now born again as a hummingbird—my beak is in the blossom! I'm a hundred acres of wheat. I've been needing some rain real bad, and now you are three days of soft steady rain. Oh, baby I used to be a ground hog, but now I'm right on the edge of becoming something else, and if you keep doing what you're doing, you're gonna have yourself one hell of a big white horse right in this bed beside you.* These exchanges might not be your idea of erotic, but just try swapping this kind of thing back and forth when you're actually in flagrante delicto. We're talking major enhancement of what was already more than acceptable!

14.

I wake to sobbing. What Is Unknown is sitting up on her side of the bed. She's trying to stifle the noises she makes with her weeping, but now she knows I'm awake. "I'm sorry," she says. She sniffles. I place my hand as gently as possible between her shoulder blades. "I hate it that everyone's afraid of me," she says. "Usually it doesn't bother me, but I dreamed people were throwing stones at me. I was buried up to my neck, and they were throwing big stones. Sharp ones. They were yelling." I stand up from my side of the bed, go around in front of her, kneel down, and take her hands in mine, put my dry cheek against her wet one. "It was just a bad dream," I croon to her. I feel her head nodding. We're quiet for a while. "*You're* not afraid of me, are you?" she asks in her faintest voice. I hold still so that she won't think I'm pulling away. "You are," she says. "I know you are." I pull her closer. "Don't lie to me!" she says.

15.

This morning What Is Unknown is apologetic. It has come to her that she needs to change sex. She says she feels herself getting a little stale. "For me it's easy," she says. "I've done it more than a few times," she says, nodding. "Not really all that big a deal—not like it is for you folks. I just have to go to this place I know and stay for a couple of weeks. It's like a retreat. Very quiet and some wonderful people to talk with about what's happening, what it feels like, what kind of new life is opening up. All new clothes, too. You probably don't know this about me, but I've always had an eye for men's fashions. Those yummy silk sports coats? And ties—God, I love ties. I can hardly wait," she says, her voice sounds downright gleeful. Then she catches herself. "I'm really sorry," she says, touching my hand. "It's not you," she says. "But it is me," I say. I do my best to keep from sounding whiny. "Well, yes," she says, "but it would be that way with anybody. So it's not *just* you," she says. "That makes me feel so much better," I say on my way to my study. I slam the door.

16.

We're on the interstate headed south to Galax to attend the Old Fiddler's Convention. We're both quiet—we know the end is coming. Miles pass. My eyes are on the road ahead; What Is Unknown stares out her side window. Then I become aware that she's staring at me. When I turn, she gives me a mischievous grin. Then quick as a magic trick, she raises up in her seat, slides her hands up under her skirt, slips off her underpants, and places them on the console between us. I'm so startled I can't help twitching the steering wheel, but after I get the car back under control, I glance over again. She's still grinning, but it's different this time—sentimental. I want to tell her that I know she did this just for auld lang syne. But all I can manage to squeak out is, "Thank you." "You're welcome," she says.

17.

I'm bereft. The awful thing is I know she could be right here in town. She could live on this block. But I won't recognize her in her man self. I can see myself one afternoon noticing a good-looking fellow in great clothes having lunch at Blue Bistro—and the more I look at him the more certain I am that I've found her. I won't be able to stop myself from going over to the table. "What Is Unknown?" I'll ask in a soft voice. And the guy—the damnably buffed out and irresistibly gorgeous stud!—will cock his head at me in a way that will be tauntingly familiar. "Excuse me?" he will say.

Scrap Wood

My sculptor friend Jim Diehr, keeping an eye out
for wood of notable character,
finds a blown-over peach tree, desires
its twisted roots, and so saws them off,

hacks them into approximate likeness,
maybe with something in the back of his mind
or maybe just absent-mindedly
recreating with some of the junk

he's collected over his years
of seeing promise randomly scattered
over the planet. My sculptor friend Jim
in his studio enters the place where mind

becomes pure spirit, so that realizing
astonishment and gratitude in new shapes
is always ongoing, even (or maybe
especially) in his dreams. It's just

what he does. These old half-mutilated
wood scraps he takes some ways toward what
they seem to want to be, then he props
them up, patiently leaning the one

against the other until they look right
enough that he can leave them. It doesn't
bother him anymore, spending time like this.
Now he can come back to them. Or not.

Dream Sender

    for Jim Diehr

Tonight you're soaring fearlessly over Prague
while speaking Portuguese with your dad,
but last night that man you never should have
smiled at lay beside you in bed touching
your left breast and murmuring, "What's your name?"

These lives I send you in your sleep are not
random—they were yours all along. I just
release them from this little box in my lap.
I congratulate you on the good run
you've been having. Others won't be so lucky.

Soon I will send out an hourglass spider
trained to crawl across someone's eyelid, a huge
savings account that will quickly dissolve
from someone's bank, and a wailing child who
can't be comforted. I love my job, I

dispense ecstasy and suffering
in equal measure, and I'm neither thanked
nor blamed. I'm God's best-kept secret—the one
who answers your deepest questions. In darkness
I whisper in your ear who you really are.

No Where

> Hopper's people have no where to go...
> —TONY MAGISTRALE

Lately I've begun mourning its absence,
that beloved *Where* that made our lives
so incorrigible, every morning sun so
dependable, kept us from doubting the truth

of spring tulips. *Where* had trees, grass, a brook
that used sunlight to make rocks pretend to be
diamonds. *Where*'s blue dome was where God hid
shyly and let third graders cherish the fragrance

of their spelling books. Oh, ever morose Hopper—
I know it's not your fault. You just discovered
those people, they were already Republican deep
in their bones, already planning to hijack *Where*,

haul it off to their grim castles, lock it up
far back in the old slave quarters, guarded
and safe, out of sight of the ten-million fools
who irresponsibly loved such dearest distance.

Genital Epistemology

1.

don't it make you snicker how desire goes
everywhere incognito undiscussed
but witnessed by every man woman and child
in a blink the mind carries out the sex
calculation *to what extent do I
yearn for intimacy with this person* I'm
seeing/talking to/playing cribbage with no
matter how far-fetched wrongful damaging
comic or impossible the results zap
through our brains level of attraction low
or high odds of it happening zero
or maybe or likely but all too often
a little secret erupts *yes damn right
I'd do that* and we take it to our graves

2.

that we had the hots for our flirty aunt
here in our town a much-admired Spanish
teacher forty-two years old mother of two
caught having sex in the back seat of her car
with her seventeen-year-old student must
have gone crazy with love lust for that boy
then there was the writer who met her
biological father when she was
in her thirties and he in his fifties
their decision to become lovers she
says came out of rational discussion
not one of us can claim we have nothing
in common with people like that between
our legs lives knowledge we can't speak aloud.

Sex Sentence

I opine most women feel
vaguely erotic almost
all the time whereas men
sporadically feel
specifically erotic
when stimulated by certain
visual phenomena
knowingly or unknowingly
created out of the vaguely
erotic (and often witty)
ladies' fashion impulses
into which I dare not delve
for fear of pissing off some
dear friends but generally
related to the subtly
revealed in juxtaposition
with the enticingly
concealed, so that in ideal
circumstances a vaguely
erotic aura engages
a specifically erotic
potential thereby
producing a sexual
combustion wished for by both
parties, though mathematically
speaking the ignition
occurs randomly more
often than by design, thus
resulting in awkward, sad,
idiotic, bizarre, unpleasant,
sometimes even felonious
behavior, the possibility
of which so discourages

women they seek the company
of other women so that
the vaguely erotic may
be safely manifested
in conversation and so
frightens men they go back
to Manland, where they hang out
with their brothers & concoct
fabulous narratives
of their specifically
erotic adventures
& astonishing triumphs.

Wren & Bear

    for Tasha Graff

Wren:
this morning I am caruso pavarroti mariah carey frank sinatra with maybe a touch of lady gaga & her cutting-edge beauty & I am loved by the sunlight the copper beech the clouds the air piano teachers & all educated citizens whereas about you they have nightmares & when they see you they don't know whether to curl up on the ground or raise their hands above their heads scream or be quiet & shiver themselves to death plus I am up here & you are down there.

BEAR:
MY GRANDFATHER TELLS OF WAITING UNDER A CEDAR TREE WITH HIS MOUTH OPEN A WHOLE AFTERNOON UNTIL A LITTLE JABBERMOUTH WREN LIKE YOURSELF FLEW INTO IT & PERCHED ON THE PINK CARPET OF HIS TONGUE & SANG A FOOLISH LITTLE SONG LIKE YOURS & SO VAIN WAS THIS WARBLING IDIOT IT REALIZED WHERE IT HAD PERCHED ONLY WHEN IT NOTICED THE PICKET FENCE OF MY GRANDFATHER'S YELLOW TEETH & THEN MY GRANDFATHER EXHALED LIGHTLY WHEREUPON THE BIRD FELL OVER UPSIDE DOWN ASPHYXIATED & DEAD & RATHER THAN CHEW UP & SWALLOW SUCH A PITIFUL PILE OF FEATHERS MY GRANDFATHER SPAT IT OUT ONTO THE GROUND & EXCRETED MIGHTILY & WENT TO LOOK FOR GRUBS BEETLES WORMS NUTS & BERRIES.

Wren:
this afternoon I am michael jackson maria callas dave brubeck duke ellington the irish tenors the mormon tabernacle choir plus a touch of lady gaga & my size song & extreme beauty were decreed by the same creature-maker who designed you to be the example of all that is crude odious dull songless fetid & brutal under the sun which has little use for you anyway look at my wings look at my wings just look plus I am lullaby hymn sonata concerto blue grass soft rock & I must remind you again because you keep forgetting how I am forever up here & you will always be down there.

BEAR:
WHAT LOVES ME MOST ARE RATTLESNAKES WHO SLEEP WITH ME THROUGH THE WINTER THE NIGHT THE DARK IN ITS THOUSAND VARIATIONS THE ROCKY STREAM THAT WOULD FREEZE YOU INTO OBLIVION IF YOU SO MUCH AS DIPPED A WINGTIP ALSO THE LITTLE FAWN AT THE EDGE OF THE MEADOW THAT DREAMS OF A FAST & SWEET DEATH COYOTES WHOSE SONGS ARE DEDICATED TO ME HUMAN BABIES BEFORE THEY LEARN FEAR DOGS WHO KNOW THEY ARE TREACHEROUS LOCKED UP IN THE HOUSES OF HUMANS AND SO NEED SOMETHING TO BARK AT TO PRETEND TO THEIR MASTERS THEY ONCE WERE WILD HIGH ROCKY SLOPES OF MOUNTAINS EDGAR ALAN POE WILLIAM FAULKNER JACK LONDON TOM WAITS MARK ROTHKO WHOSE PAINTINGS ARE SECRETLY DEDICATED TO ME CELLISTS TUBA PLAYERS ROCK & ROLL BASS PLAYERS SHOSTAKOVICH & MOST KINDS OF BERRIES.

Bear Goes Metaphysical

If I'm not a bear, thought the bear—
and wistfulness rose in him, *maybe*
he was a falcon, a redwood, a slug,
a raccoon—but then his bear brain
made him look down at chest and belly,
and what he saw—his furry paunch,
the queer white of his skin, a tick
so full of bear blood it would soon
drop off—was like a boulder blocking
the path of his thinking. *A soft*
little spring breeze, he thought, why
couldn't I be the high meadow full
of quarrelsome bobolinks who nip
the little yellow moths from the air
when they're hungry? Why couldn't I . . . ?
but suddenly such mental bearfoolery
sickened him into standing humanlike
to bam his ribcage with his front legs,
and to angrily stomp (though he hated
when he split infinitives) Lady Fern,
Guelder Rose, and Carpet Moss until
he'd dampened his lower paws with black-
green juice, conjured a rich forest dirt
and vegetable stink to waft upward. Oh,
that was when the bear got it straight,
not just the news of his irrevocable
bearness and the pissant misery
of a bear's lot but also on the other
hand the luck of his snout, his tongue,
his penis and balls, his improbable speed,
his forever hidden-from-himself asshole,
his being no other creature or thing
than the bear that he was, an aging

and otherwise unremarkable eastern
black bear. He was never to be a brown
trout married to icy water and speckled
slithering among stones, nor could he be
the red-tailed hawk whose killing ways
were, to the bear in his picture of it
right then—death falling from the sky—
so merciless, clean, and righteous.

Bear and the Crows

So many in the winter trees they caw
they swirl all through the blood-orange light
Bear can't decipher what they're telling
though it's him they're squabbling over
him stronger than ever as night sifts
down on him like rain in these woods Bear
invisible to himself he must be lost
which is why he stands still now why
he sways clacks his teeth woofs at the crows
but doesn't move he's so strong now he's not
concerned about stupid crows he could climb
that ash so fast he'd swat them from the sky
if he wanted to no bear is ever lost
even if he can't find his way back to where
he was sleeping before the dream woke him
sent him stumbling out into snow so deep
Bear thought he was dead in his dream that's what
he was now he sways clacks his teeth woofs
at what it felt like in his dream so weak
he couldn't move with that stink like crow sound
he sways in the clearing woofs urinates
a long time soon the dark will make the crows
shut up and fly to their nests Bear will
not bawl like a cub stuck in a tree he
will stop clacking his teeth stand still for soon
a small fox will come sit down some way off
wait like a stone to see what Bear does next—
at dawn Bear will kill it in a flash crunch its
bones in his teeth leave shards to show every
idiot crow he is not lost just stronger.

God Speaks of Dancers

Their quest—what does the human body mean?—
must be carried out without understanding,
so I love them for their blithe ignorance,
I admire the balls of their feet, their horse-
sturdy buttocks, the stink they make falling
in a pile of wet flesh at the end of the show.
Their laughter then so pleases me, they may
misbehave as they wish, and for that, too,

I love them. That naughty one named Elise,
who claims she's the best goddamn dancer of all,
who pulled up her dress to display her lack
of shame? I grant her long life, no illness,

a clear mind, much mischief, no need to pray,
and no fear of me. Get out of her way.

The Dancers Speak of God

> *And David danced before the LORD with all his might*
> SAMUEL 6:14

If God didn't love us more than She does you,
we'd be with you down there numbing your asses
in the dark watching us up here with our flesh
giving light a good name. When a hawk flies,

that's just normal weather, but when a girl
flings her pretty sack of bones across a stage
God sucks in Her breath and sends a tornado
to ravage Alabama. That's special—

and with it goes obnoxious. God likes
us best when you can hardly stand us. Who
thinks God's a sweetie grew up in Disneyland.
You want to know why we get to prance through

our lives like the Lipizzaner stallions?
God wants to love human flesh. It's not easy.

How It Works

Picasso would sometimes make art on his plate
with the bones of the fish he'd just eaten—
which historical precedent explains
my inclination to reconfigure
dining room chairs around the table,
gewgaws on the piano top, magazines
on the coffee table. That multicolored
armadillo, the small dome-shaped blown-glass owl,
the metal spidery thingamajig
that when wound up will dance spastically?
They have their exact places in my house.
If this poem is not a masterpiece,
some heedless grandchild must have disarranged
my quartz lizard, stone bird dogs, painted heron.

Sit With It

want to make something out of nothing got
to sit with a soup of vague thoughts images
jittery words agitating to line up
direction not yet clear destination
mostly unknown got to forget spouse kids
email newspaper even that book you love
that's lighting the path toward a death
you can live with got to sit still and try
to believe something's somewhere in this non-
profit time-wasting sandbox full of cat
-droppings something that wants to fork lightning
down from your brain up from your heart even
a whisper out of your soul assuming you
have one which maybe this morning you don't.

The Greatness of Teddy Wilson[1]

David Lehman, in his deftly short poem
"Radio," says "the greatness / of Teddy Wilson /
'After You've Gone' / on the piano"
gives him pleasure and comfort.
                                       I thank David
though I wonder if this song and all New
Orleans-born jazz is not a sly critique
of slave-made culture, which is to say whitey's
ways.
           Don't Wilson's fingers speak his mind?
While you generate misery so you can wallow
in wealth, I make joy of such intelligence
you can grasp only the part that doesn't
tell of suffering,
                     the meanness of the world
you're making or what fools you are to love
music that hopes to God you'll soon be gone.

---

1. *The Writer's Almanac*, November 7, 2013.

Practice

    for Jack White

Reek of valve oil, stink of reeds and spitty
brass when we lifted our horns from their cases,
discord beginning with *squeak bam blat thump honk*—
we'd warm up even making our way to our seats
with cacophony swelling toward crescendo
until Mr. White reached the podium
and tapped the music stand with his baton.

Backs straight, waiting in a half circle, a hundred
kids with clarinets, trombones, French horns, saxes,
trumpets, tubas—then snares, bass drums, tympani,
and cymbals: When that man lifted his baton,
we obliged him with the ridiculously gorgeous
noise of our growing up. Sometimes he'd smile,
sometimes whisper, *Oh kid, play that horn, make me cry.*

3
The Bat

The Call

Flying toward my house this morning the geese
send out such a racket that almost without thought
I set my laptop aside, stand up, and step quickly

out onto my porch—then out onto the grass. In cool
air I raise my face toward their clamor: low
overhead, wings whistling, their bellies golden

in October light, thirty or so that sound
like hundreds generating a sociable ruckus
in complaint or praise of the great seasonal

upheaval dispatching them wherever they're headed.
Then—and this is the luck a day will sometimes
grant me, a wish I haven't sense enough to realize,

a random perfection—in utter silence a turkey vulture
sails across even lower than the geese and at an angle
near enough I see how its flight feathers shift. This

is not about the chill that shivers me
when the geese and the majestic scavenger
have passed, not about my desire to return

to my work and my computer, the warmth
of my house or my soft sofa. It's about
that half an instant of standing alone

under a sky the blue of my infant dreams,
among the trees gone yellow and orange, the still
air clear as a soprano's hitting and holding E

above high C with the day just begun and the whole
raw world summoning me to step through a door
I can't even see.

Evidence Contributing to a Late Illumination

   1.
Photo of my father, wire-rimmed glasses,
only son, nerd prince—his mother, grandmother,
tighten his tie, pat his jacket, comb his hair,
advise him not to marry Mary Frances.

Photo of my mother, age maybe sixteen,
Lace-collared polka-dot dress so proper
but still showing the source of her power
over those old ladies—she can have babies—

and how they must have loathed the child! Her arm
around my mother's waist, Great Grandma Lawson—
complainer and snuff dipper—might smile if
only she could push this brat bride off a cliff.

My mother's face shows she knows it and won't
run from rage wrapped in manners like a present.

   2.
Though she lived only minutes, our oldest
sister was named after her grandmothers,
who detested each other. Her stone offers
one date for the birth and death of Ida Grace.

Mother was seventeen then. Last year moved
by desire, this year it had to be something else.
The rest of her life she woke to loss, then got
sent to bed at night with its bitter kiss.

Charles came along and stayed alive, two years
later there I was, then Bill. Never another

girl, just boy, boy, boy. The later pictures
show her as still proud but a little forlorn—

photos of a face concealing how much it hurt
wanting a daughter, a lifetime half-thwarted.

Even Then I knew

    for Lisa Fay Coutley

Our mother was often desperate
because of my brothers and me—once

she threw the dish drainer at Charles,
slapped the back of Bill's head so that

his face plopped down into his spaghetti,
and what did she get for that? More boy

guffaws in our victory over her self-control.
Our mother wore little mascara, served her sentence

of three sons in a house at the end of a dirt road
in a time of no Post-it notes, two channels on TV,

no shrinks, no antidepressants, and her only role model
was Mrs. Perkins, who one afternoon rode Toby's bicycle

down Church Hill, skirts fluttering over her thighs,
to buy a six-pack of Pabst Blue Ribbon. Decorum

meant everything to our mother, and if someone had told
my brothers and me that mothers can drive away,

that would have frozen us in place like a game
of statues before Charles would have said, *Oh yeah,*

and where would she go? and Bill would have said, *Maybe
down to the post office?* And me? I'd have been

scared, because I loved her way more than my Roy Rogers
silver cap pistols with their white fringed holsters,

but finally I'd have found something real
funny to say.

Meditation

As my mother did I sometimes stand
at the kitchen window thinking nothing
in particular. My view is of the back
of an apartment building, my mother's
was of our garage and driveway, the two
of us studying nothing very interesting.

I can't know about her because she died
when she wasn't much older than I am now—
but these never-planned occasions never
fail to please me, to improve my mood.
Sometimes a bird will shoot by, a student
come out to sit on the steps and smoke.

I imagine she saw rabbits and robins,
occasionally a stray dog or barn cat.
People didn't often appear back there.
But here's the point—in such moments
whatever one sees is just what one wanted
all along and not because it's special.

When my friend in Roanoke, needing the usual
sight of her side yard, saw instead a cow,
she called her friend in Washington to ask
his advice, and he—a city fellow—advised
her to call the police. Believe me, that
was not what she wanted, a fugitive cow.

And yet if my mother had seen it, a smile
would have come to her, she'd have gone out
to shoo it away. If she'd known whose cow
it was, she'd have called that house to ask

them to come for it. She'd have savored
the episode and called me to tell about it.

This is not about pleasure, which is nothing
special nowadays anyway. A sunbathing girl
once fell off the roof of that building
and broke her arm, and I'm glad I didn't
see that. I just want ordinary twilight,
somebody picking a guitar in the distance,
maybe a gray horse if there's one available.

Epiphany in the Parking Lot

Shut up our mother said we couldn't say,
so behind her back we said it all the time,
risking her witch's look, the hairbrush,
or a talk from our father, whose sadness
we exacerbated with our acting up, not that
he much cared what we said to each other
but punishing his sons wasn't what he wanted
after working all day and so it was a failure
of strategy on our part to provoke our mother
to have to ask him to talk to us about *shut up*
or the picture I drew of turds dropping
from a stick man's butt or Bill's tantrum
in front of Miss Ossie Price, but I still can't
get the words out, something shuts me down
when I'm around somebody who needs to hear it—
yesterday morning I saw this girl get right
in a guy's face in the City Market parking lot,
they were smoking and kind of stepping around,
when she shouted, "Shut up!" leaning into him,
grinning and red-faced as if what he'd said
was so damn scandalous but perfectly delicious
like *I know you're not wearing underwear today*
or *blankety blank blank,* and God did it hit me hard,
sixty-five years old, both parents long dead,
and whatever that girl was feeling right then—
which had to be some fantastic amalgam of arousal,
embarrassment, shame, and joy—wasn't anything
I'm ever going to feel, even if I get another
sixty-five, even if I ever do break through
and finally ask some jackass to please be quiet.

Dog Sutra

    for Bishop, Henry, and BooBoo

When I've lived with dogs dogs have taught me not
to admire myself so much. I've got a bad
temper, when I'm angry I'm a bastard,
but if the dog is tactful I can be
manipulated—e.g. don't sit and stare
at me when you want to go out, that'll just piss
me off. Instead, do your downward dog stretch,
wag your tail, and bark politely.
                                        Dutiful,
I scooped your poops with plastic bags, walked you
at least once a day, and never forgot
your food and water. I even talked to you
while I cooked dinner.
                                    I miss your complex
fragrance and witty ways, but my new dogs
are duty free—Mostly Alone and Empty House.

Okay #2

I never loved anybody I didn't
also not love; therefore, I've always thought
I had a treacherous heart, which I'll never
stop thinking. This morning, though, I think love
that's easy is a Hallmark card from your dead
grandma, love of no currency.
                                            The not
love's got to be defeated day in, day out,
welcoming back home the daughter who spat
in your face and slammed the door on her way out,
picking up the still-wasted son from detox.

What's ultimately romantic? Kissing an old
spouse with a paunch and stinky breath. Can you
do that and mean it? Well, no, but that's exactly
where the love lies that you can take to the bank.

Against Auld Lang Syne

> Is it relevant to remember old times...
> or should I move forward?
> —MARK MULCAHY IN AN NPR INTERVIEW

At seventy-one I've got syllables—
unabashed wallowing in nostalgic
sappiness—and years ago I learned
contempt for "Auld Lang Syne" playing in bands
at New Year's Eve parties where liquored-up
old couples sloppy-smooched while they tried
to dance without falling down. Seventeen,
wearing shades, juvenile skinny, I was way
too cool for such squalid scenes.
                                                I flee
my past not for crimes or even shame but
for fear it's out to steal my future. Silly,
I know, to believe I have to stay alert
for some splendid possibility waiting
out there for me to snatch it up. It's
not like I don't have it in me to stumble
over and ask you to dance. *Not to worry,*
I'll slur. Prop me up, and I'll hold you tight.

My Father Breathing

for Charles R. Huddle, Jr., 1911–1986

The hundred-yard uphill walk from the highway
to our house used up most of his smoker's wind
so that he had to gather himself not to show
our mother how exhausted he was when
she met him at the door for a quick kiss
and to take his dinner bucket and thermos
to the sink then hand him the toddy she'd fixed.

Doctors warned him and though he tried he couldn't
quit—he'd started smoking when he was twelve—
and so to be near him was to hear his
inhaling and exhaling. A slow mean death
finally stopped his hard work, but now I hear him
in my own chest, that involuntary song
our hearts and lungs make, one breath to the next.

Witness

1.

A boy I studied my grandfather,
who'd lived many a life before I even
slipped into this world. I now understand
that old man to have been a kind of text
that taught me about my future—either
I'd drink hard from twilight into full dark,
spend hours by myself in a dim room full
of books reading under a yellow light,
seek out the company of illiterate men,
remember odd anecdotes from my past
to tell visitors, and speak fondly
of kind waitresses in towns I'd come
to know in my youth, or I would be
another kind of man altogether.

2.

Jehovah's Witnesses made grandmamma
angry just by knocking on her door, so
she went upstairs while he welcomed them in.
Those Witnesses stayed for hours—most people
willing to talk to them did so briefly
through their screen doors, whereas he,
having no opinions on Armageddon,
inquired as to where they were from, who their
father was, did they have brothers and sisters,
and had they ever been to Kingsport, Tennessee?
Good times with the ladies was what I think
he'd loved as a young man, and conversation
was something my grandfather still enjoyed—
even if it was with strangers and small boys.

A Little Drunk

Five and already
a pretty good sneak
with an appetite
for things I wasn't
old enough to want—

e.g., opening
the whiskey bottles
in my parents' stash
in the old sideboard,
sniffing the fumes

until the room spun
like a carousel—
this night my parents
entertained guests
and turned the kitchen

table into a bar.
So after dessert
while they sat talking
over their coffee
I excused myself

and wandered the house
ignored and bored
out of their sight
opportunity
presenting itself

behind a closed door
our breakfast table
now offering me

bourbon but I chose
scotch and turned it up

for a sip that shocked
me with its sizzle
in my mouth and throat
made me blink back tears
but then pleased me too—

alone as a ghost
with grown-ups sitting
so close I could hear
the mannerly tones
of each word they spoke.

I'd done something wild
and true and without
anyone knowing.
I even walked back
through the dining room

past parents and guests
an invisible
slyly bemused
secret-savoring
boy with a flushed face.

Giddy as I was
I sat eavesdropping
on them some minutes
then stood up to get
more of that feeling—

power or maybe
irony, something

grown-up, a grown-up
way of knowing things
children couldn't grasp.

I'm an old man now
and can't know my thoughts
or feelings in those
moments of whiskey
washing through my five-

year-old brain. Sometimes
I ask myself if
I was abnormal
or just your basic
inquisitive kid.

The question *What is
wrong with me?* never
quite leaves my thoughts.
This morning I'm by
myself eavesdropping

on the world chasing
a secret feeling
that I can savor
entirely within
my mind my body

the human machine
keeps itself busy
with projects that lead
to pleasures of one
sort or another—

in my case now it's
these words but back then
it was one sip more
of that feel-good juice
that would make me bloom

into brilliance
the likes of which no
grown-ups had ever
witnessed. Well yes now
I see I wanted

their admiration—
not so different
from what I hope to
gain now from lining
up these syllables

and just as foolish
a project. All right
we know how this tale
ends—boy stumbles
into dining room

pukes everywhere
in his mother's lap
on the table cloth
monstrous embarrassment
company can't leave

fast enough nothing
to be done clean him
up put him to bed
now I lay me down
to sleep but no good-

night kiss no mention
of the episode
next day or ever
again my whole life
as if if we just

packed it in enough
silence we could make
it go away. Which
mostly worked—they're

all dead and I'm not
the alcoholic
they probably
thought I'd become—*they*
being my parents

and their guests that night.
I don't often drink
whiskey my habit
is two beers a night.
My doctor thinks one

should be my limit.
I still ask myself
What is wrong with you?
Mostly the answer's
Nothing much. But some days
it's *Everything!*

Then

When my mother was the age I am now
she entered a phase of sweetness and stayed
there maybe two or three years. She'd finished
grieving for my father, she wasn't lost
the way she was when my brothers and I
married and made our homes elsewhere, seemed free
of those rages that scared us as children.

When my mother was the age I am now
she treated us boys, our wives, and our kids
like new friends she wanted to please. She'd sit
on the porch to watch us play family
croquet, applaud or sympathize like the god
we hoped watched over us, the god of now
I lay me down to sleep. This was years ago.

Real Lady

Fifteen years after her death, as if I need
to be reminded, people tell me that's
what she was. A high school classmate who had
little use for me back then will say, *Your
mother was a real lady.*
                            Are they whispering
the answer to that impossible math problem
I've spent my whole life trying to solve?
She had a bad temper, I could say. *Snobbish,
vain, quick to judge—she stopped speaking to her
sister for marrying a widower too soon
after his wife's death, didn't even attend
her sister's funeral.*
                  All of which,
I guess was part of being a real lady.
My nod doesn't say much. Or explain why
their words fill me with such yearning and grief.

The Uplift Obligation

Okay, death's our destination so we need
pleasure, comfort, and distraction to help
us accept our upcoming oblivion.

When Kezia in Katherine Mansfield's
"At the Bay" tells her grandmother, "You're not
to die," the old woman remains silent.

The scene ends with the child and her grandmother
tickling each other until they've forgotten
what they were talking about. There must be

a thousand ways to take our minds off death—
tickling, of course, picnics by the river,
pictures, stories, sex, music, family dinner,

and aren't we kind to smile, speak cheerfully,
then tuck our children in and kiss them goodnight?

Comes a Moment

—and it must be like the one when you decide
it's time you had sex for real, or the one
after you've got a spouse, a kid, and a job

when you see how your life's going to be
for the next three or four decades, and you tell
yourself, *Okay I've got to make this work,*

or maybe like the one when retirement looks
like an opportunity for sweeter days
so you say, *Yes, I'll take it,* but this one

feels scarier than all those others put
together, your eyes, ears, lungs, heart, mind
even your bones are all chanting, *Gotta do it!*

—and you have to say, *You all go ahead, I'm going
to sit here and rest awhile, don't wait for me.*

Homothology

Bird bams window behind him,
startling a Jesus out of him,
so he stands, steps out, finds
a fist-sized finch knocked still,
scarlet neck dangling its head
in the slot between bench slats.
Our man's partially evolved
empathy kicks in, along with
some guilt—his feeder summoned
the bird to his porch—and a desire
to hold so small a thing. Ever so
carefully he lifts the finch,
feels its life flicker, little
flame about to sputter out, cups
the bird between his palms, softly
thumbs its chest to jiggle its heart
to keep the beat. What's a finch
to a man? What's a man to a finch?
Two-way dime-a-dozen. The man sits
on his bench, mindless as the bird
warming in his hands. Wits absent,
maybe coming back sometime soon.

When the Bat Goes to Live with Jesus

Only God and the bat know why
a bat wants entrance to a human
house, but a human can come to
understand the bat just wants out:

It flutters through hallways
and rooms, swoops up and down
staircases, makes us cringe
and yelp, use tennis rackets

to try to kill it, pillows to
to knock it down, but eventually
we feel the creature's panic—
poor thing is trapped and lost.

Killers a moment ago, now we're
inept bat-escape enablers,
but really there's little we
can do beyond opening windows

or doors and hoping it finds
its way out. In the waiting
time we sit still and watch it
circle chandelier, dining room

table, kitchen island, rising
and falling, fluttering as it
searches through our living
space that is its living hell.

When Emmylou Harris sings
"When He Calls," her voice

glides into *I'm going to live
with Jesus* with such rapture

I feel my own eyes flutter
in the ecstasy of being carried
home, not sitting here watching
the Pacers-Heat game on ESPN but

my other home, that sweet night
I came from, the one the bat
suddenly discerns and swoops
a foot above the floor, just

beneath my 50-inch flat screen,
out the door into the cool May night
of trees, stars, and sky. I nearly
swoon I so love the instant.

www.ingramcontent.com/pod-product-compliance
Lightning Source LLC
Chambersburg PA
CBHW030123170426
43198CB00009B/714